Jack a

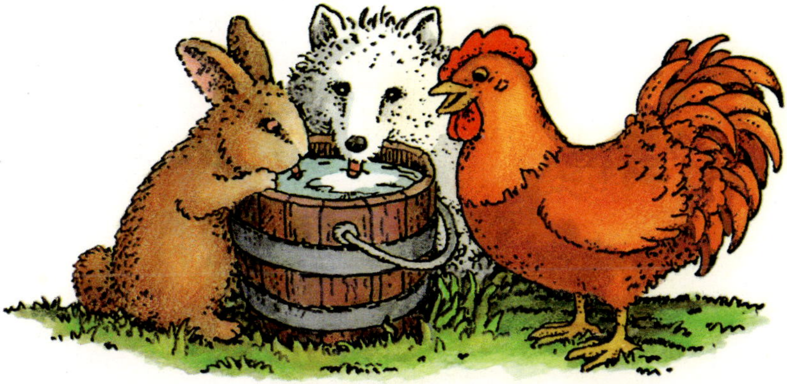

Illustrated by Sharleen Collicott

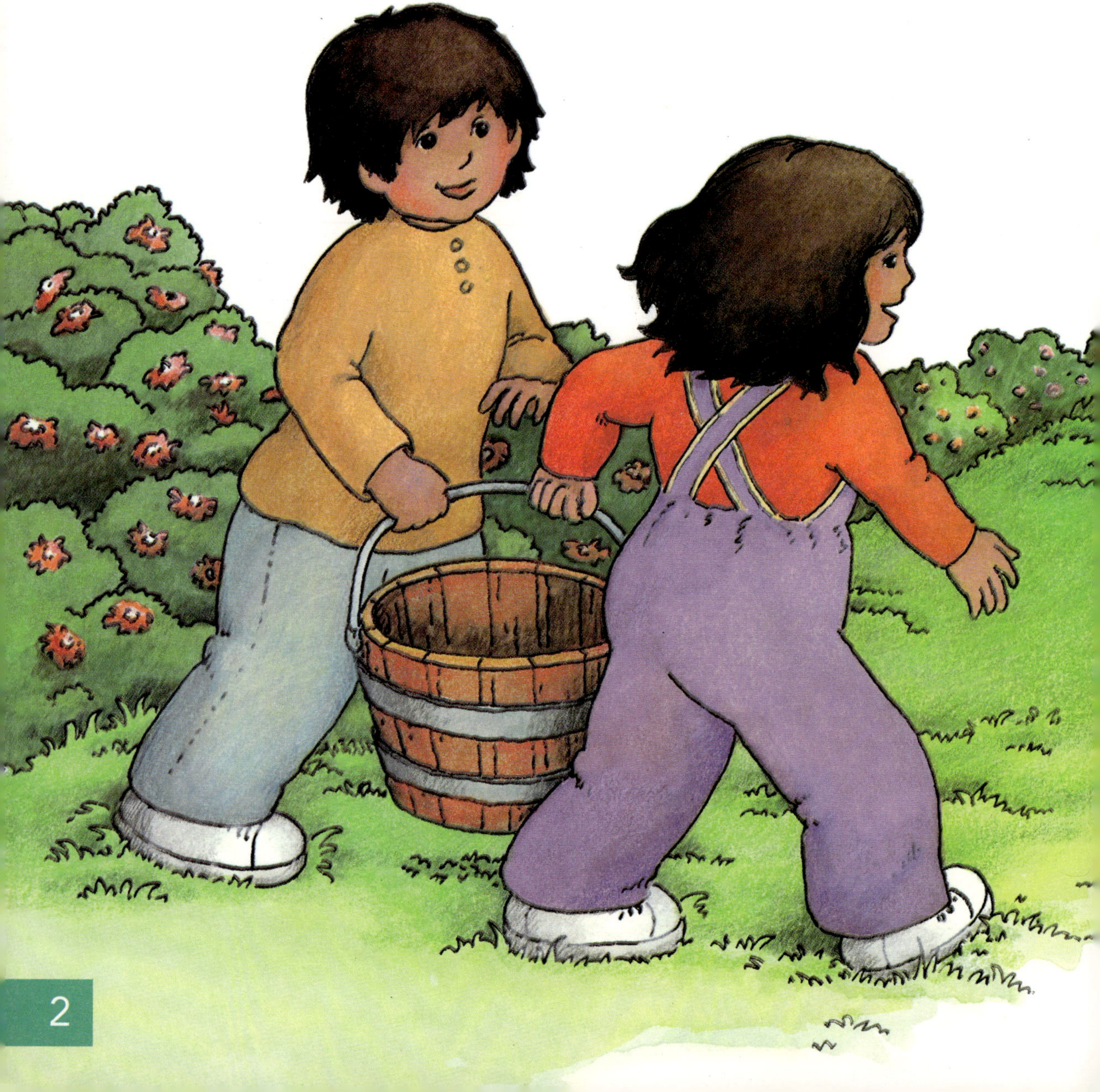

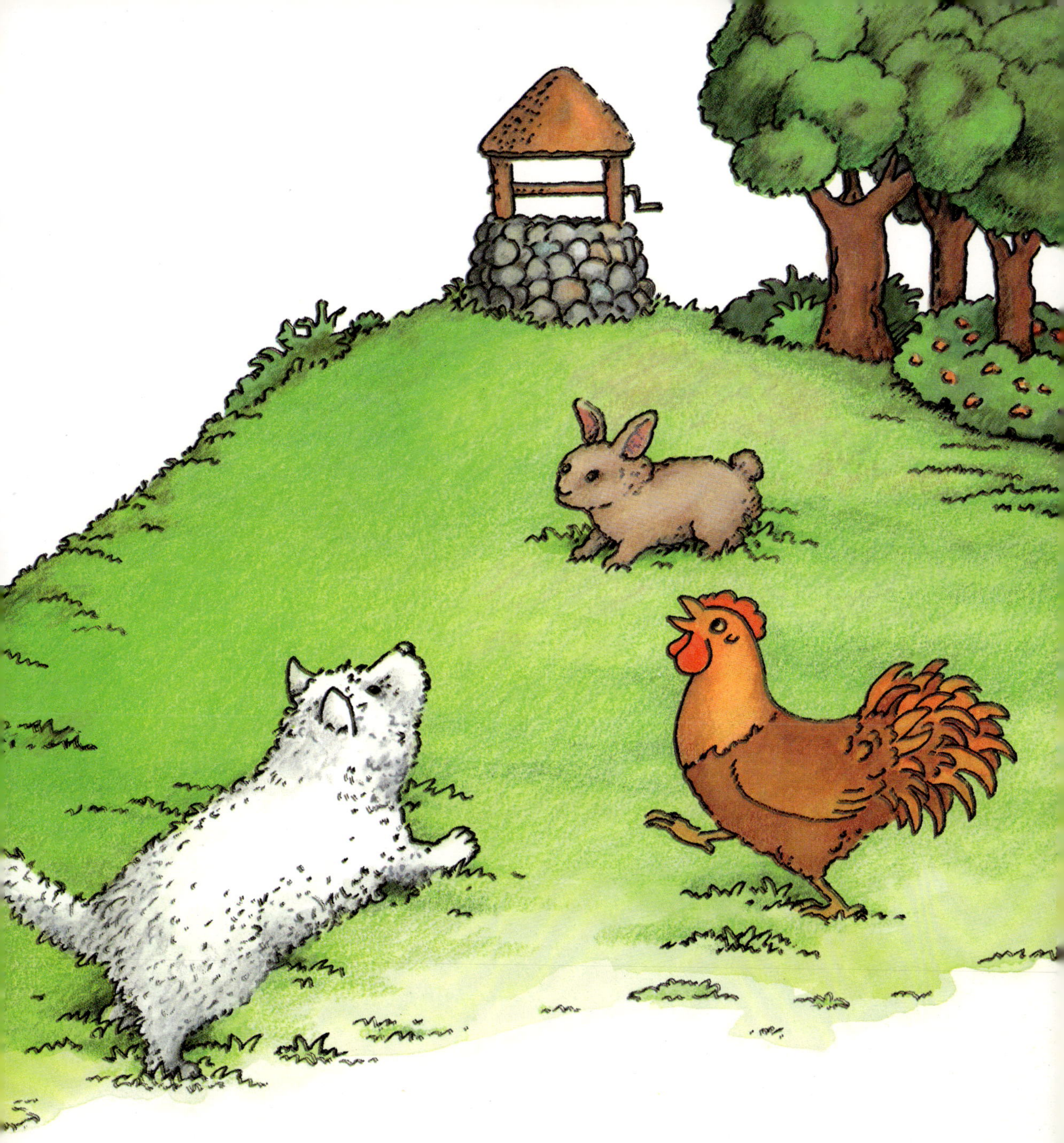

Jack and Jill went up a hill,

To fetch a pail of water.

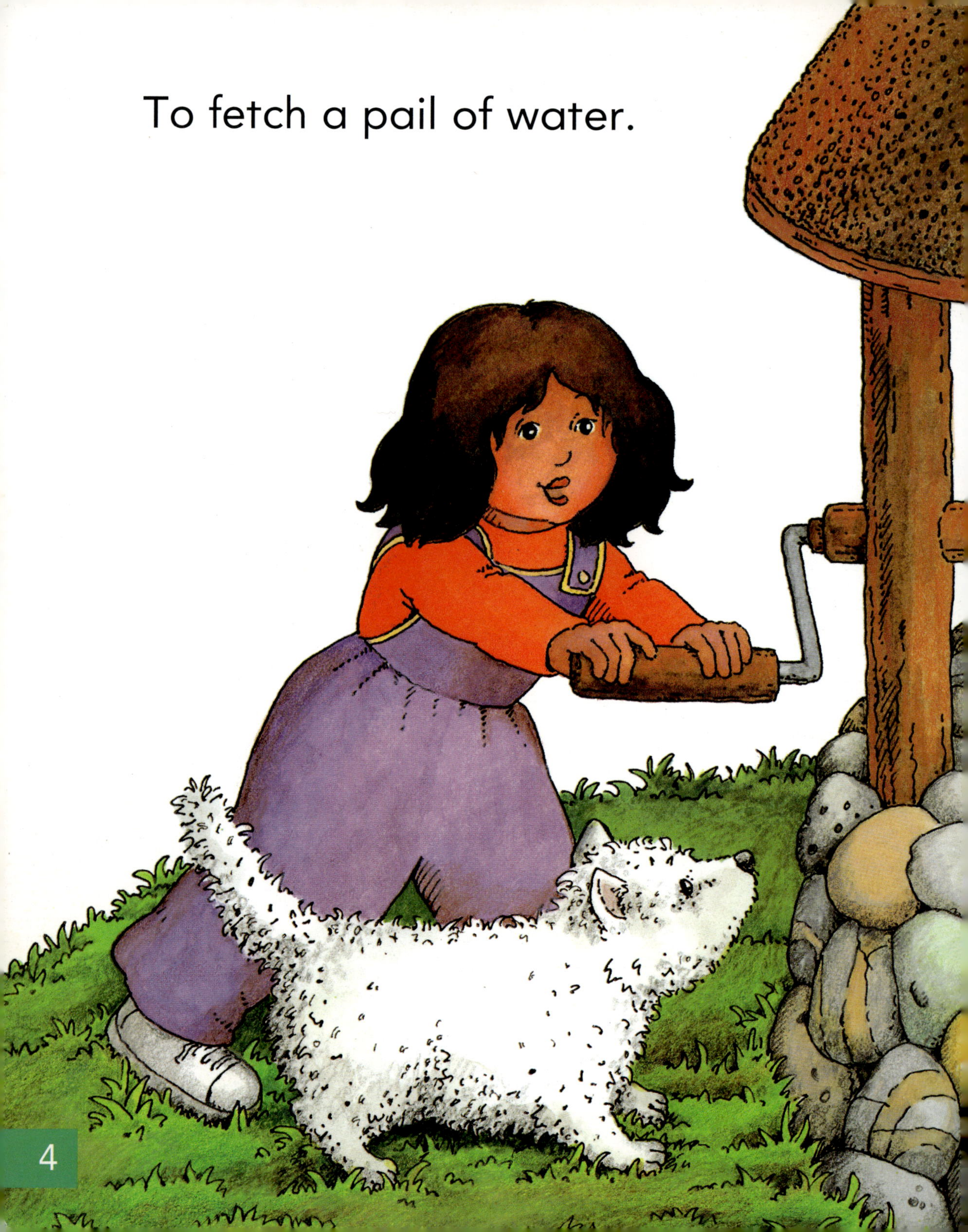

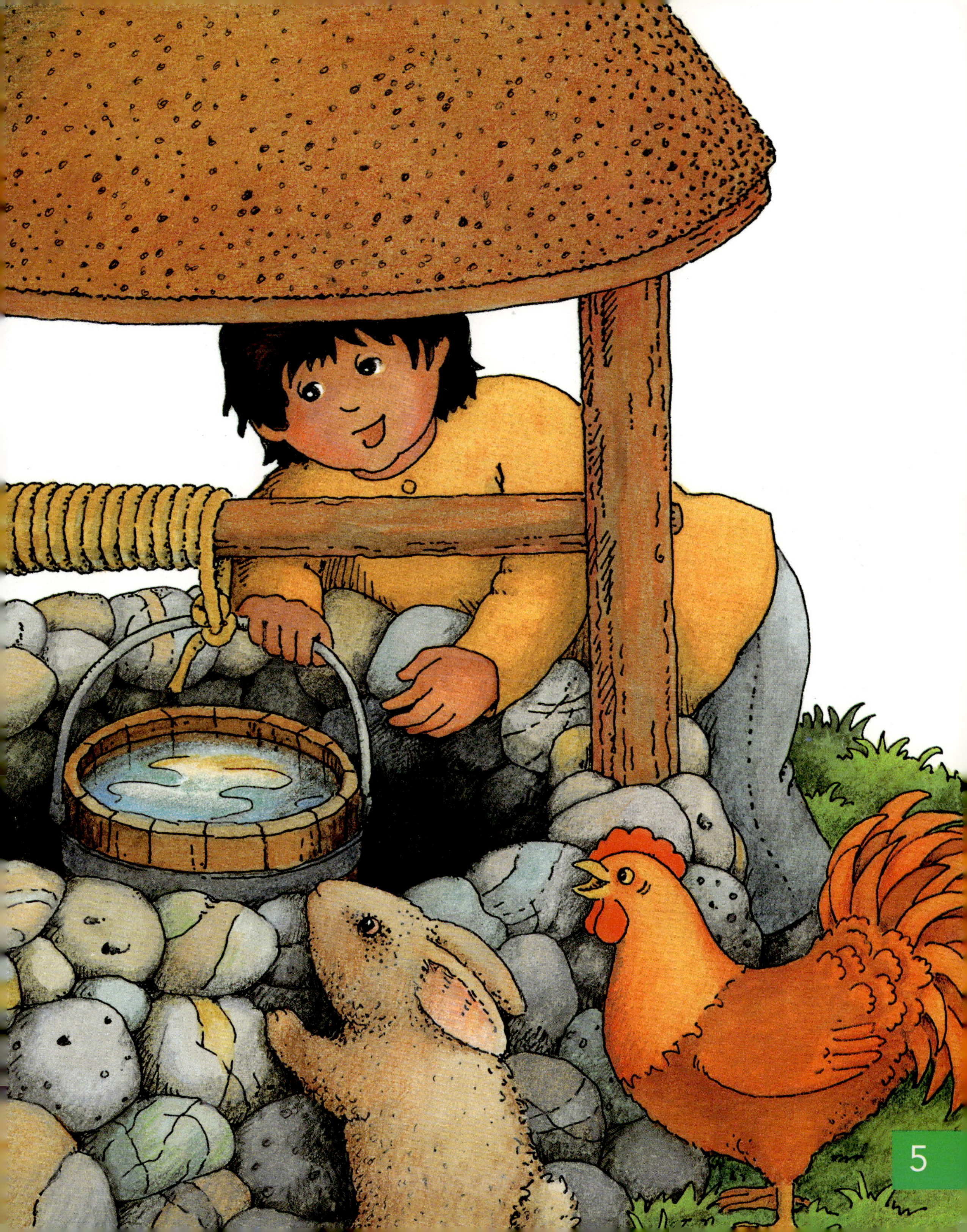

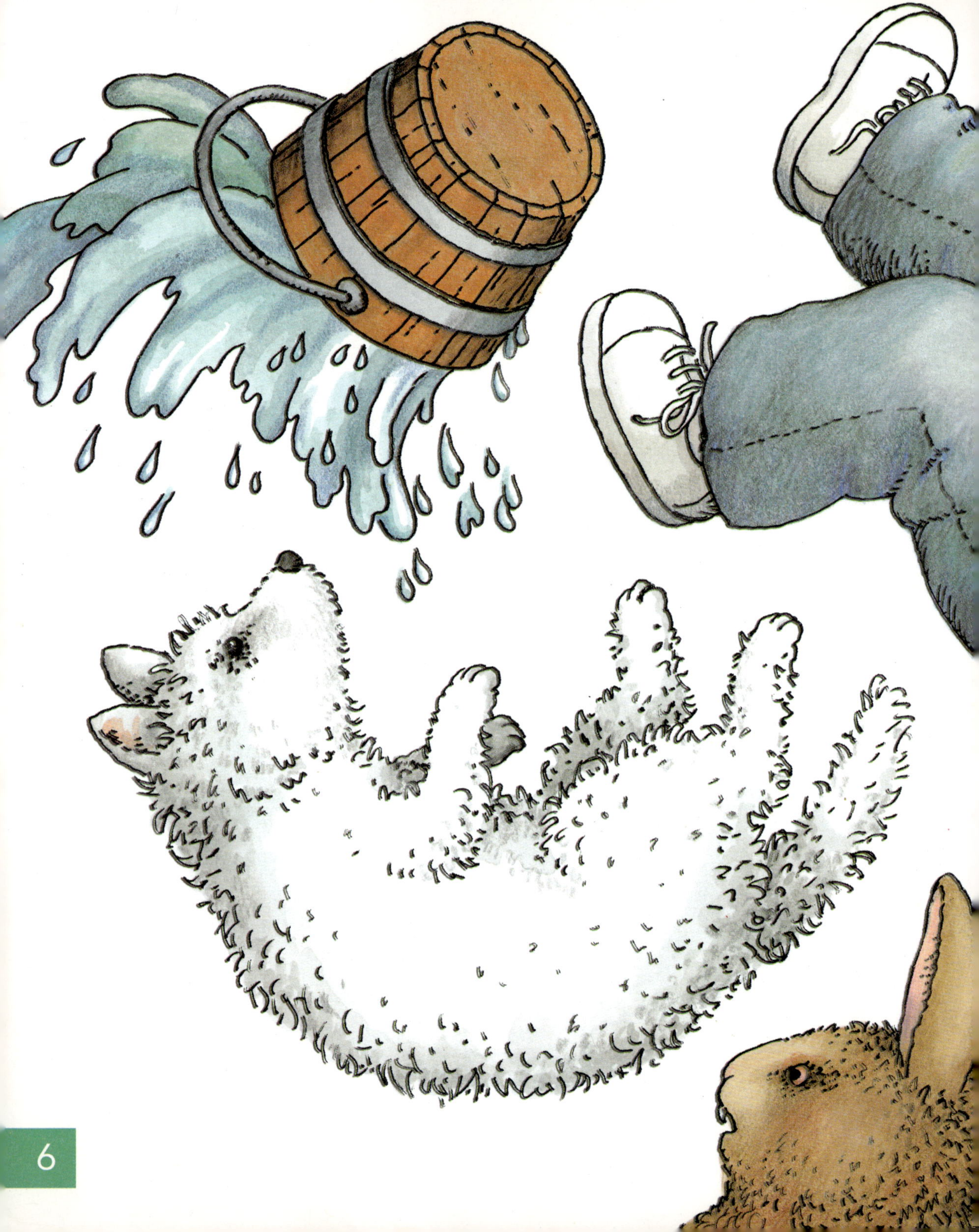

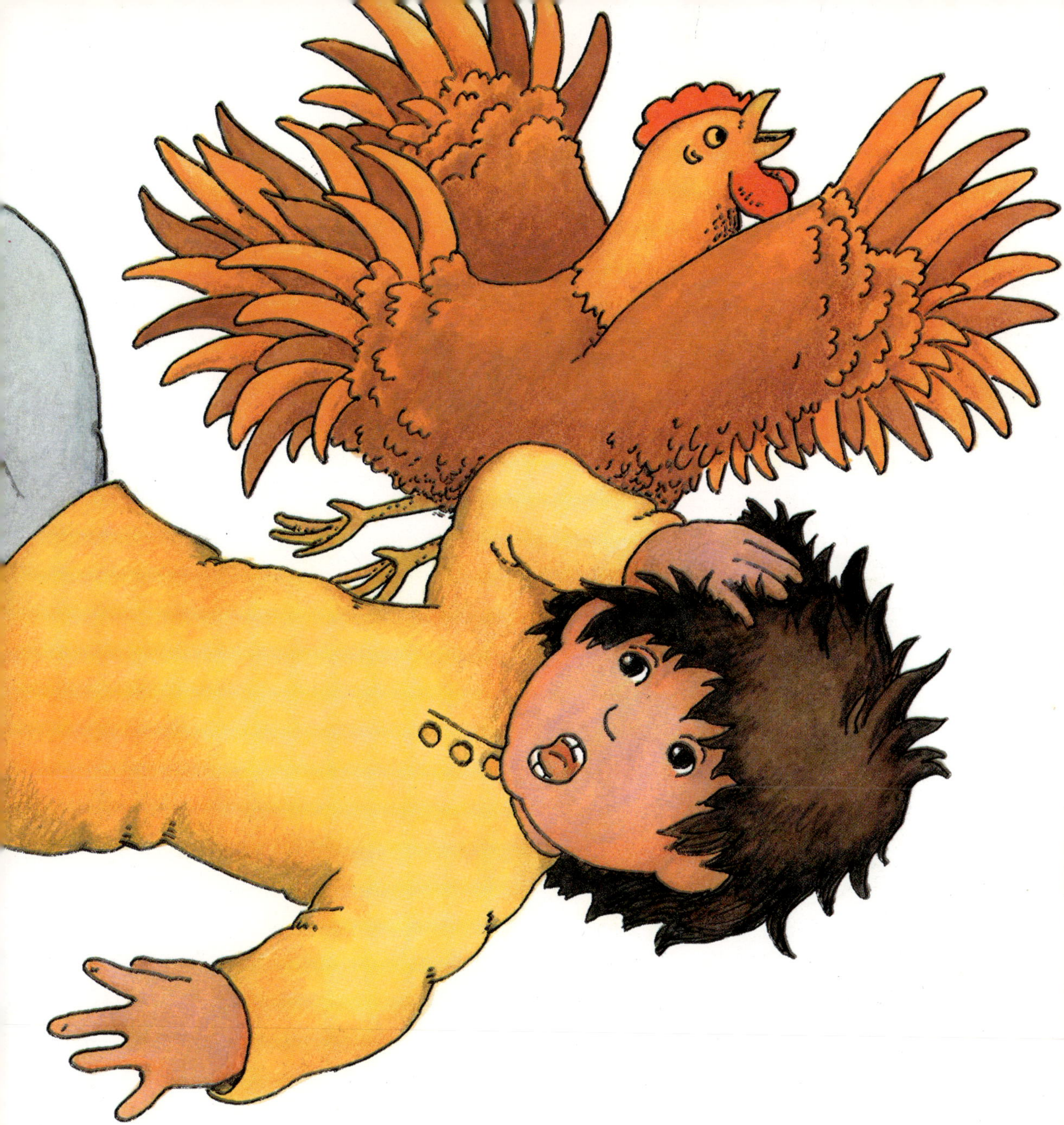

Jack fell down and broke his crown,

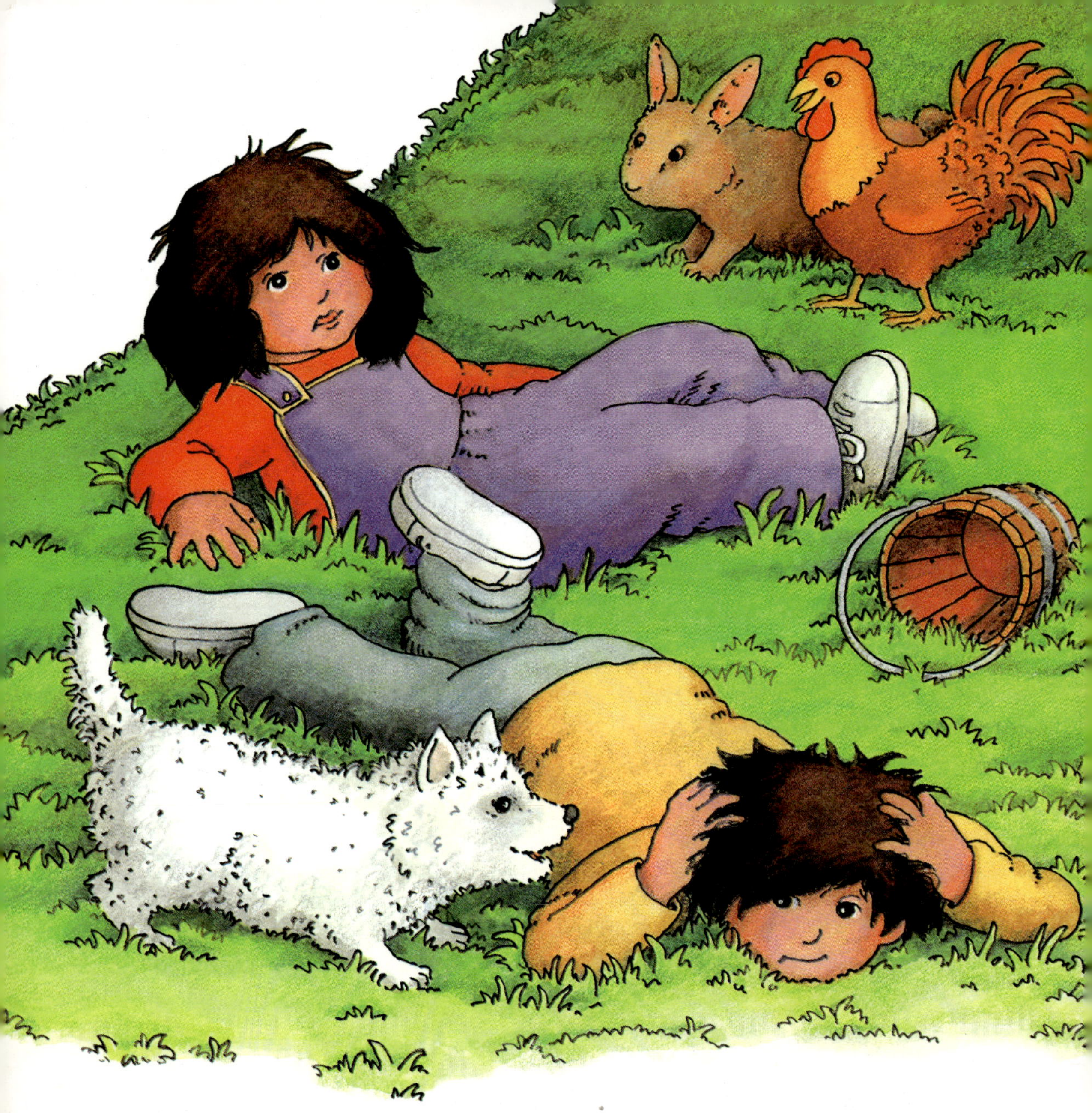

And Jill came tumbling after.